Following Ben

Expository Preaching as the Power for Frail Followers of Pulpit Giants

Michael A. Milton, Ph. D.

With introduction by
Dr. Ben Haden

Faith for Living
Bible Messages

Wipf and Stock Publishers
Eugene, Oregon

Wipf and Stock Publishers
199 West 8th Avenue, Suite 3
Eugene OR 97401

Following Ben: Expository Preaching as the Power for Frail Followers of Pulpit Giants
By Michael A. Milton, Ph. D.

1st edition.
Printed in the United States of America

ISBN 13: 978-1-59752-958-7
ISBN 10: 1-59752-958-3

Faith for Living
Bible Messages

The booklet you are reading is part of a series of Bible messages. This message was delivered on March 11, 2004, at the National Conference on Preaching, Southern Baptist Theological Seminary, Louisville, Kentucky. Each message in the series is designed to address theological issues in the Bible that need to be translated into a "faith for living." It is my belief that all theology is, ultimately and necessarily, practical. Theology that is not practical is not a theology rightly applied. For all theology must, as Dr. Robert L. Reymond says, "pass a radical Biblical muster."

> All Scripture is breathed out by God and profitable for teaching, for reproof, for correction, and for training in righteousness, that the man of God may be competent, equipped for every good work (2 Timothy 3:16-17).

In *Following Ben* I pray that God will encourage you as you guard the treasure that is entrusted to you.

This little booklet is dedicated to the glory of Jesus Christ and produced in honor of the congregation I serve at First Presbyterian Church of Chattanooga, Tennessee.

Introduction

By Ben Haden

I followed a legend! My only other church was small; this one was substantially larger. My other church was modern, poor, and unpaid for; this one was the oldest organization of any type in the city, affluent, and paid for. The legend wore a morning coat; I wore street clothes. He had been there for years and was beloved; I was new, totally different, and highly secular.

When any pastor follows any man in a church, he is automatically confronted by a different culture of that congregation, their interests, their challenges, even their language.

I hugged Mike Milton and helped install him as the new senior pastor. I was leaving a church with a unique history; I knew Mike Milton was entering a church with a unique future. I determined spiritually and ethically to pray for Mike Milton, not to look over his shoulder and not to second-guess anything he did.

The value of this booklet is to alert every pastor moving to his first or different church to stop, think, pray, and ponder what he is getting into. No two churches are the same. The spiritual condition is not the same in any two churches. The needs are not identical in any two churches. Budgets are not identical in any two churches.

It is so easy to forget that a believer must have a call from God to be a pastor and then a completely separate call from God to go to a particular church.

The wonderful key to any new church is not the pastor who preceded you, but the Jesus you followed in coming there.

Following Ben

Expository Preaching as the Power for Frail Followers of Pulpit Giants

In 1 and 2 Timothy, we read about a great concern of the Apostle Paul, given to his son in the ministry.

> Timothy, guard what has been entrusted to your care. Turn away from godless chatter and the opposing ideas of what is falsely called knowledge (1 Timothy 6:20, NIV).
>
> That is why I am suffering as I am. Yet I am not ashamed, because I know whom I have believed, and am convinced that he is able to guard what I have entrusted to him for that (2 Timothy 1:12, NIV).
>
> Guard the good deposit that was entrusted to you — guard it with the help of the Holy Spirit who lives in us (2 Timothy 1:14, NIV).

Guard the good deposit. What is the "good deposit?" It is, of course, the apostle's doctrine of Acts 2:42.[1] It is the gospel of grace that Paul labored for and defended in Acts 15 and in Galatians. It is the Word of God.

Guard this Word of God. This is my concern, and if you are a pastor, this is your concern. This concern of Paul's, and mine and yours, is given in the context of following one who has kept it. In other words, the "good deposit" has made it through one pastor and is now, like a distance runner handing a baton off to another runner, being entrusted to you. What are the implications? How is this to be done? How can we guard the deposit in our generation?

[1] They devoted themselves to the apostles' teaching and to the fellowship, to the breaking of bread and to prayer (Acts 2:42, NIV).

Timothy

Have you ever seen the old Disney children's movie *Dumbo*? In that quaint old movie is a scene of the circus parade coming to town, and you see the elephants, linked nose-to-tail, forming an unbroken chain of giants. But what is really funny is not just to see a smaller giant named Dumbo linked up to this chain, but at the very end of the parade of giants is a little mouse named Timothy, hanging on to the tail of the elephant. I feel like saying, "Hello. My name is Timothy! I am a mouse following a parade of giants, and I probably need therapy!"

I followed one of the most extraordinary church orators in the twentieth century. Ben Haden was (is) an amazing speaker with a one-of-a-kind delivery, a worldwide television ministry, and an amazing pastoral record. He served this church faithfully for over thirty years. There are stories all over town, all over the country, about the homiletical and pastoral feats of my esteemed predecessor. I knew I was following that giant, but little did I know that there had been a veritable pastoral parade of pulpit pachyderms in Chattanooga for over a century and a half!

Before Ben Haden was a Dr. Fowle, who wore a morning suit replete with Edwardian tails. His voice boomed biblical exposition in our sanctuary for thirty-eight years. During the week, he taught Bible at the University of Chattanooga. He was renowned for his city ministry. Hospital wings and entire buildings are named for him. I was told that he never took a salary but gave it all to the church. I always squirm when I hear that one.

Before him was a man who was a great scholar, Dr. Venable, who died five years into his pastorate. His son, who is eighty years old, is my clerk of session, and I am pastor to his grandchildren and great grandchildren.

Before Dr. Venable was Dr. Bachman, who served for fifty years. He was a former moderator of the old Southern Presbyterian Church and was named the Chaplain of Chattanooga. He also distinguished himself as a chaplain in the Confederate Army. He was, moreover, a leader in academics and a leader in the community. He dedicated the cornerstone of our present historic downtown church by depositing into it, literally, the Westminster Confession of Faith and catechisms, the hymn book, the minutes of the General Assembly of that year, the rolls of missionaries supported, and the membership roll of our church at that time. He was a man bigger than life in many ways. His opening prayer for the sanctuary is engraved in marble over the portico of our church building. He always wore a clerical collar. I have a picture of him fly fishing, and he still had a collar on. I read that he never turned off the light on the porch of the manse for the same reason that he never took off that collar—he wanted to always be available and wanted the church to know that a minister was ready to meet their spiritual needs.

Before Dr. Bachman, was a Dr. McCallie. If there is any question as to his pastoral legacy, you need only look at the street sign. Our church sits on McCallie Avenue. He and his sons founded a school in Chattanooga—The McCallie School for Boys. During the Civil War, when every other minister left the city during the occupation of Chattanooga, Dr. McCallie stayed, ministering to both Union and Confederate troops.

I could go on. But suffice it to say that all of the eleven pastors before me were godly, powerful, and noted for their holiness and their faithfulness to the Word of God. When you walk through the foyer just outside our sanctuary, you are overwhelmed by the larger-than-life oil paintings of these great men of God.

When I was called to this venerable pulpit, Mae and I were introduced to the officers, and they presented me a crystal that reads, "To Michael Anthony Milton, 12th Senior Pastor in 161 Years." I accepted it with humility, but also with fear. The words made me feel small and helpless. I have a friend who often says that he feels like Barney Fife in the presence of John Wayne. I felt that way as I came into this pastorate. At times, as I move from my study to the sanctuary on Sunday mornings and pass through the hall of heroes, I still feel that those grand oil paintings of those holy men of God are hovering over me with a stern look, reminding me not to goof up what they worked so hard to build! I know my sin. I know my limitations. How can I follow Ben Haden, Dr. Fowle, Dr. Venable, Dr. Bachman, and Dr. McCallie? More than that, I had heard the horror stories of following in the footsteps of famous, long-tenured pulpiteers. In fact, when I was called to the church, many of my friends, like Bildad and Elihu, questioned whether God was smiling on me or judging me. Even my old mentor, Dr. D. James Kennedy, under whom I completed my internship for the ministry, reminded me that it is a hard thing to follow a great preacher. Perhaps he will remind the man who follows him of that observation.

You are saying, "So you've followed a tall steeple man. What is that to me? And how does your experience and insights impact my ministry?" Your pastorate may be different—in context, in size, larger, smaller, or different in many things. However, there are things in this matter that concern all of us. Aren't we all following in a line of godly preachers? And who among us feels worthy of the task of standing between God and man, announcing God's Word to men and standing with men and women to petition God for help in their time of need. You may not follow Ben Haden (who, incidentally, has been wonderful to me), but you do follow Spurgeon, Luther, Calvin, Wesley, Whitefield, Edwards, and the college of preachers who stretch across denominational and ethnic lines all the way back to Paul, John, Moses, and our Lord Jesus Himself.

All of us come with questions about our pastorate:

- How can we be faithful in our ministries?
- How can we have a ministry approved by God?
- How can we have an effective pastorate?
- How can our ministries, our preaching, support church health?
- How can we have power in our ministries?

There are significant answers to those questions that can be located in the Bible and cultivated through prayer, study, consecration, and dying to self. I want to consider one single answer, and I want to answer, without apology, from the Word of God—2 Timothy 3:16-4:1-5. There, a little pastor named Timothy (just like the name of the mouse in *Dumbo*), who followed a ministry giant (a pastoral pachyderm named Paul), is instructed on how to latch on to the legacy.

> I charge you in the presence of God and of Christ Jesus, who is to judge the living and the dead, and by his appearing and his kingdom: preach the word; be ready in season and out of season; reprove, rebuke, and exhort, with complete patience and teaching. For the time is coming when people will not endure sound teaching, but having itching ears they will accumulate for themselves teachers to suit their own passions, and will turn away from listening to the truth and wander off into myths. As for you, always be sober-minded, endure suffering, do the work of an evangelist, fulfill your ministry (2 Timothy 4:1-5).

Let's just say it and let the power and the possibility for failure sink in—Timothy was pastor of a church which was planted by Paul. When I feel really challenged, I think of Timothy. The elders at Ephesus had fallen on the neck of Paul and wept over his departure at Miletus. Three years of powerful ministry gave Paul the right to call them to shepherd the church of God which had been purchased with His own blood. Paul, in his swan song at the twilight of his remarkable ministry, reminded Timothy of how he had to follow Jesus Christ. He gave the secret to power. He lifted a mouse…no, his words were so divine and powerful that they magically transformed the mouse into an elephant, a giant linked to his ministry and linked to Jesus Christ, powered by Almighty God Himself. What did Paul commend? He commended the Word of God, and after calling it God-breathed, he charged a God-called man to preach. The answer to the question, How do mice latch on to elephants? is neither original nor surprising at this conference. Like Charles Hodge addressing new students at old Princeton, I, too, say to you, "I glory in saying that you will learn nothing new here." It is an answer that every frail follower of pulpit giants must remember: The only way for a mousy man like me to follow a giant like Ben Haden is through expository preaching. The only way for any of us to stand in the long and honorable legacy of gospel preachers is through expository preaching.

Why? I offer eight concise reasons why expository preaching is the power for the pastorate, whatever your situation.

Expository Preaching Is the Power of the Pastorate because It Is Divinely Wrought.

The way for Timothy to take his place as the beloved child of Paul,[2] to latch on to the legacy of faith that dwelt first in his grandmother, Lois, and his mother, Eunice,[3] to fan into flame the gift of God[4] which was transferred through the apostolic laying on of hands of Paul himself,[5] to overcome a spirit of fear,[6] to guard the good deposit entrusted to him,[7] to teach others what he has learned from Paul, thus extending the apostolic succession to another generation,[8] to avoid getting entangled with civilian pursuits,[9] to proclaim and teach the whole counsel of God, from the old covenant to the new covenant,[10] for the sake of the elect that they may obtain the salvation that is in Christ Jesus with eternal glory, to take his place, to flee youthful passions and purse righteousness,[11] and to do all of the things he is charged to do at Ephesus, like reminding the saints not to quarrel about words,[12] to avoid irreverent babble,[13] to correct his opponents with the aim of leading them to repentance and a knowledge of the

[2] 2 Timothy 1:2
[3] 2 Timothy 1:5
[4] 2 Timothy 1:6
[5] 2 Timothy 1:6
[6] 2 Timothy 1:7
[7] 2 Timothy 1:14
[8] 2 Timothy 2:1
[9] 2 Timothy 2:4
[10] 2 Timothy 2:8-13
[11] 2 Timothy 2:22
[12] 2 Timothy 2:14
[13] 2 Timothy 2:16

truth[14] so that they may avoid snare of the devil.[15] To say it again, the way to be this man and conduct this ministry is *khrucon ton logon*—to preach the Word.

Paul makes it clear that the Word of God alone is able to meet the mission of the preacher. The reason is that the Word of God is the authoritative instrument from the throne of God to accomplish God's mission in the world. We remember that Paul's admonition to preach the word follows his teaching that "All Scripture is breathed out by God and profitable for teaching, for reproof, for correction, and for training in righteousness, that the man of God may be competent for every good work."[16] Paul had been building up to this in everything he had written previously.

I love the way Dr. Robert L. Reymond puts it: "the Bible is a Word from another World." In his *New Systematic Theology of the Christian Faith*, Reymond writes, "When God gave his Word to us; he gave us much more than simply basic information about himself. He gave us the *pou sto* ["(a place) where I may stand"], or base that justifies both our knowledge claims and our claims to personal significance."[17]

The Word of God is the place where the pastor may stand. Indeed, our very existence, our calling, our vocation only has meaning through this Word. I recently read J.C. Ryle's *Warning to the Churches*,[18] in which the old Bishop of Liverpool warned his diocesan ministers of the perils they faced. The book left me amazed at his prophetic gifts and understanding of the times. I do not have such gifts, I am sure. But I do want to raise a danger related to the matter before us.

We live in an ever increasing iconoclastic culture that demands image and entertainment to communicate, that tells the preacher that short sound bytes are more persuasive than exposition of a text, that narrative is more important than the exposition of a text, that postmodern man cannot endure direct teaching but needs to make the homiletical turns for himself. I say that this is a danger to the preaching of the Word, to evangelism, and to discipleship. In the midst of such an age, we would all do well to remember that God called for Israel to do something that the heathen did not do: to think about Him in His Word, not in image. The late Neil Postman, a non-practicing Jew, saw this clearly. The God of the Jews was to exist in the Word and through the Word, an unprecedented conception requiring the

[14] 2 Timothy 2:25
[15] 2 Timothy 2:26
[16] 2 Timothy 3:16
[17] Robert L. Reymond, *A New Systematic Theology of the Christian Faith* (Nashville, TN: Thomas Nelson, 1998), 111.
[18] J.C. Ryle, *Warnings to the Churches* (Edinburgh: Banner of Truth Trust).

highest order of abstract thinking. Iconography, thus, became blasphemy so that a new kind of God could enter a culture. People, like ourselves, who are in the process of converting their culture from word-centered to image-centered, might profit by reflecting on the Mosaic injunction.

The Word, my beloved brothers in the ministry, is the God-given place where we may stand, where we may reason, where we may dialogue with man. Indeed, we have been forbidden to go elsewhere. As a pastor, the reason I want to focus on expository preaching—that is, proclaiming the inerrant and infallible Word of the living God as it is written, as it has been transmitted to me by God through the church, passing muster with the intent of the author, with conviction in my own life, and with love for those before me—is because expository preaching fixes itself, by its best definition, onto God's Word, divinely wrought and divinely authorized. This has powerful implications for my ministry that I want to explore further.

The only way for me to stand in the company of pulpit giants is to stand with this Word from another world. The truth is, if they are truly giants in the church, if they are linked from Spurgeon to Ryle to M'Cheyne to Whitefield to Bunyan to Luther to Calvin to Wycliffe to Augustine to Paul to Jesus and the prophets, then they are men of this one Book, and that is all they have to say.

Expository Preaching Is the Power of the Pastorate because It Is Biblically Faithful.

We have seen that Paul tells Timothy to preach the Word, and we all know why. Preach the Word because the Word is divinely wrought. It is God's Word, and what could be nobler? If there were no other reasons to proclaim His Word than the mere fact that the Bible is His Word, that would be enough. The matter then becomes, How shall we do it? To preach the Word must be to faithfully communicate that Word. Expository preaching, properly understood and properly done, fulfills this mandate.

Expository preaching is, as our host Dr. Al Mohler put it in his contribution to *Give Praise to God: A Vision for Reforming Worship*, "Expository preaching is that mode of Christian preaching that takes as its central purpose the presentation and application of the text of the Bible."[19] If expository preaching is really ex-

[19]R. Albert Mohler, Jr., "Expository Preaching: Center of Christian Worship" in Philip Graham Ryken, Derek W.H. Thomas and J. Ligon Duncan, eds, *Give Praise to God: A Vision for Reforming Worship* (Phillipsburg, PA: Presbyterian and Reformed, 2003), 112.

posing the mind of God in a given text and communicating the mind of God to men and women, then no other methodology will do.

William Temple was not an expository preacher, though he said enough good things that we often quote him. But the old Bishop of Canterbury did not believe that God would communicate His Word propositionally in the Bible because man could not understand it even if He did. Temple did not believe in the inerrancy and infallibility of the Bible. Temple did believe that you could understand what he wrote; otherwise, he wouldn't have written anything, but that is another argument.[20] Enough to say, if we believe that the power for our ministries is the Bible, as Paul teaches us, then it surely follows that expository preaching is the only model we should seek in communicating that Word.

As an adjunct professor who gets to teach preaching every now and then and as a pastor who gets to mentor younger preachers before sending them to other places of service, the subject of the future of expository preaching in light of post-modernity and post-Christian America is a hot topic. I have found that many are wrestling with the question of whether such communication really can reach across the widening and ever-changing rivers of modern culture to reach the hearts of an emerging generation. The realities of the emerging generation cause them to question expository preaching, and in fact, have led several on a journey to "find their voice," as they tell me. I'm happy to say that many of these with whom I have met have worked through that question to rediscover the power of expository preaching for this generation.

The whole matter of whether expository preaching can effectively communicate to a postmodern, post everything generation (as Tim Keller calls our times) is a question that has been answered time and time again. If we are preaching the very Word of God, then surely God knows what we need in every age. This Word worked in the fallen ruins of Eden when God promised a Savior in Genesis 3:15. This Word worked in Genesis 12 when God promised Abraham a land, a nation, and a blessing that would reach around the world. God's Word was enough in 586 BC in the crumbled remains of Jerusalem when a weeping prophet named Jeremiah preached through tears. God's Word worked in first century Rome when Paul preached it. It worked in the eighteenth century in America when George Whitefield roared out its truths up and down the colonial coast. It worked in Korea in the nineteenth century when missionaries

[20] See Robert L. Reymond's discussion of Temple and his position in Robert L. Reymond, *The God-Centered Preacher: Developing a Pulpit Ministry Approved by God* (Fearn, Ross-shire, Scotland: Christian Focus Publications, 2003), 11

preached there, and it worked in industrial Dundee, Scotland, when Robert Murray M'Cheyne preached there. It worked in the twentieth century, the bloodiest century in the world's history, when modernity overtook the West and men such as Martyn Lloyd-Jones thundered from a world capital such as London. And it will work in the twenty-first century, in postmodern and post Christian North America, and it will work in China, Africa, India, and Bulgaria. The Word will work in Chattanooga, free slaves to sin in Miami, give abundant life in Los Angeles, renew cold-hearted saints in Des Moines, restore marriages in Peoria, reunite severed relationships in Louisville, sprinkle the spirit of holiness in New Orleans, call new missionaries out of Kansas City, and save souls from hell in Bangor, Seattle, and Paducah. The power of our ministries is expository preaching because, if what we have to say is the Word of God, how we say it matters. Expository preaching, rightly followed, is the way to say it.

I have said that expository preaching is powerful because it is the Word of God and it is faithful to the Word of God. Let me continue with my reasons why it is the power for the pulpit, but let me be thoroughly pragmatic about it.

Expository Preaching Is the Power of the Pastorate because It Is Pastorally Effective.

If this is the Word of God—and it is—and if expository preaching is the biblically faithful method for giving out this Word of God—and it is—then it surely is the key to success in the pastorate.

What do I mean? I surely don't mean to imply that success and effectiveness in the pastorate is to be connected with being a celebrity or selling books or gaining fame. This past week I read a fine sermon from 1857 by J.C. Philpot about the ever-present temptation of pride and vainglory among preachers. I am aware that each of us deals with this in some way, but no, I'm not talking about that. I'm talking about effectiveness in what I call the essentials of the ministry—gathering, growing and sending forth strong disciples of Christ. I have in mind the work of seeing souls saved, lives transformed, marriages saved, young people's hearts burning with zeal for Christ and His kingdom and desiring to die to themselves to live for Christ. I have in mind strengthening the things that remain[21] and ordering our churches according to God's intentions. I have in mind speaking peace into a troubled, maybe even splitting, congregation. I have in mind being pastorally effective in shepherding the flock of God

[21] Revelation 3:2

over whom God has made me an overseer. There is no program, no model, no paradigm, no experiment, no policy, and no amount of pure elbow grease or mental genius that can equal the power of the Word of God preached. It accomplishes everything I hope for in the ministry. Recently, someone said that the best time-tested discipleship tool in the history of the church has been morning and evening worship where there is expository preaching. My own experience as a disciple and a pastor is that I couldn't agree more. I believe that this is so.

When I counsel people in trouble, I always ask if they are sitting under the expository preaching of the Word of God. I'm not asking them to come to my church, though I would love to have them. I'm simply saying that they must locate a place to belong, a local congregation where the preacher is committed to moving sequentially through the Word of God—that may be moving through books, chapters, or other preaching portions within a book—in such a way that they are getting the mind of Christ in the study. Expository preaching is pastorally effective.

Expository Preaching Is the Power of the Pastorate because It Is Vocationally Satisfying.

When I say "vocationally satisfying," I am speaking to those who have come, in their own lives, to say with Paul,

> For if I preach the gospel, that gives me no ground for boasting. For necessity is laid upon me. Woe to me if I do not preach the gospel! (1 Corinthians 9:16).

If we are called by God to preach the Word of God to a dying world and if preaching is unveiling the mind of God for man in this Word and this is what expository preaching is, then it follows that we will only be happy in our work if we are doing that!

Eugene Peterson is the pastor's friend in so many ways. I have greatly benefitted from his various works. In *Under the Unpredictable Plant*, he tells how he was at the point of burnout at Christ the King Presbyterian Church in Belaire, Maryland. He was going from board meeting to board meeting, doing this and that. As a pastor who has planted two churches—and Peterson's church was a church plant—I know how it can be. This tired pastor went to his session and told them that he couldn't go on. He thought he was at the end of his pastorate. Fatigue is physical exhaustion, and we all get that. Burnout is a loss of meaning, and we do not necessarily have to have that, but this was apparently what Peterson had. His Session was wise and told him to list the things he went into the ministry to do. He listed preaching, visiting the sick, sharing the gospel, and the things that the Bible teaches us is our work. His Session told him, "You do those things you were called to do, and we will do the rest." You probably have read what happened. He not only was renewed in his ministry, but he also stayed over thirty years at that church.

Many of us have been greatly blessed by *The Purpose Driven Life* campaigns in our congregations. We need a purpose driven pastorate, also. If God has called you to preach, He has not called you to be a rush chairman, a religious store manager, or even a really great storyteller. Yet, there are many who will tell us that expository preaching is not enough. Peterson says, "Propagandists are abroad in the land lying to us about what congregations are and can be. They are lying for money. They want to make us discontent with what we are doing so we will buy a solution from them that they promise will restore virility to our impotent congregations. The profit-taking among those who market these [programs] indicates pastoral gullibility in these matters is endless."[22]

Let us not be gullible. Expository preaching fulfills God's purpose for our lives as preachers. He has called you to preach the Word, and you will never be happy until you go to that Word, live in that Word, exegete the meaning of that Word, dive like a Pacific native to the bottom of the ocean for the rich pearls of that Word, and then come back up from your time in the deep-blue of God's presence, string those pearls together in a sermon, and put them on the neck of your people.

Only a preaching method, a preaching approach, that is radically Word-centered, Christ-centered, gospel-saturated, and uncompromisingly faithful to the text will give you joy. For you were made to preach.

Expository Preaching Is the Power of the Pastorate because It Is Eschatologically Useful.

When I say eschatologically useful, I am saying that expository preaching brings our people into contact with ultimate realities. In personal eschatology, expository preaching prepares our people to not only live but to die. Oh, if we could hear the stories of faithful preachers who have shared those sweet and sacred moments of vigil with a family when a loved one is going home. The

[22]Eugene Peterson, *Under the Predictable Plant*, (Grand Rapids: Eerdmans, 1992), 17-18.

power for your ministry at that time is in the exposition of the Word. An elder in our church who recently went home to be with the Lord said, "I have been waiting for this. I am ready to go home." This attitude comes from expository preaching.

Expository preaching also is eschatalogically useful in that it brings our people to see God's ultimate cosmic realities. I would say that faithful exposition of the Word would probably distance our preaching from some of the excessive, eisogetic propositions that we sometimes hear at certain prophecy seminars that lead to theological speculation and seem to draw cosmic curiosity seekers. But faithful exposition, say of 1 Corinthians 15 or Ephesians 1, leads our people to see that God is a teleological God, that this world is going somewhere, and that we who are God's children are destined for something greater than ourselves.

The revelation of God gives meaning, purpose, context to time, space, and eternity, to man and God. It gives meaning to sickness, hope, and even happiness in the face of theodicy, and the questions of suffering.

Expository Preaching Is the Power of the Pastorate because It Is Personally Edifying.

The call to preach the Word is a blessing. Each week we come to the text, and we are fed by it, hopefully, before we give it to others. I know the warning in James 3 against being teachers, but we also know the words of Paul: this Word will "make you wise for salvation.[23] We will save ourselves as well as those who hear us.

I must say this, also. When we are about the work of expository preaching in the pastorate, the work carries us along, in a sense. Week-in and week-out, we develop a discipline of study, for to preach the Word of God line-upon-line, precept-upon-precept, demands time, struggle, and prayer. I know that in this room, your heads and hearts are turning, perhaps not over this address, but over the portion of Scripture that you must deliver this week. Is there anything as rewarding in life as unburdening your soul in that movement when you approach the sacred desk and open the Bible? Expository preaching feeds my soul. I know of no other way to put it. But more than that,

[23] 2 Timothy 3:15

Expository Preaching Is the Power of the Pastorate because It Is Constantly Challenging.

To present the mind of Christ in a text requires much of us, does it not? I once heard a preacher say that every time he preached, a little piece of him died. I am sure there are those for whom that is true because they are tired of preaching or they know that they will get ripped to pieces at the front door of the church. But this man was speaking about preaching in a way that I can identify with. To preach the mind of God, to go through the necessary steps to get there, then to emotionally discharge the holy calling on your life through the act of expositing a text is the most challenging thing in the world. It takes your very life.

I was once in a seminar with Dr. D. James Kennedy where seminary students were able to ask him anything they wanted. One asked, "Dr. Kennedy, what is the most challenging thing you have ever done in the ministry?" His answer was, "Prepare next Sunday's sermon." Can I get an amen on that? We all know it is true. We all know that such rigorous preaching cut short the life of John Calvin. It must be balanced with recreation and separation unto God in quiet prayer and reflection. We all know that to constantly face the Word of God each and every week, sometimes three or four times each week, is overwhelming at times. But for those called to do so, it is a response to a calling to an amazing love that demands our soul, our life, our all. Would you really want it any other way?

Expository Preaching Is the Power of the Pastorate because It Is Always Contemporary.

When we go to the Word and preach the Word, we never have to worry about whether it is the right time or if this is the right message. Surely wisdom is needed to discern between preaching Lamentations at a wedding or Leviticus 15 and "bodily discharges" at the dedication or baptism of an infant. You know what I mean. As I think about this conference, I am reminded once more that expository preaching is always in vogue, always "cool," if you will, for the human condition remains the same in every age.

Conclusion

How did Lloyd-Jones follow Campbell-Morgan? Expository preaching. How did Boice follow Barnhouse? Expository preaching. How did Timothy follow Paul? "Preach the Word." We must guard what was deposited to us with expository preaching. We must because we can't conduct a sound ministry of visitation of the sick and dying without it. We cannot carry on the work of evangelism, discipleship, world missions, building up our saints, or being a witness to our communities without expositing the Word from another world. We were made for it. It is our lives. It is our heart. Readers of the stories of great missionaries will recall the amazing story of that intrepid Scotsman, the physician Dr. David Livingston, who, like Lloyd-Jones, was not only a medical doctor but also a preacher of the gospel. You will recall that David Livingston's body was returned from Africa, where he died, to be buried with highest honors in Westminster Abbey. But do you also recall that before his body was removed from the deepest parts of that great continent to make the seven-hundred-mile trip to the coast, the tribesmen of the place where he died so loved this man that they removed his heart from his body and buried it in great ritual in the land where he preached the gospel?[24][25] Jesus said, "For where your treasure is, there your heart will be also."[26] The tribesmen knew that David Livingston's treasure was Africa. His soul would go to His Savior. His body would return, for the time being, to his native country. But Livingston's heart was in Africa.

Do our people know that we treasure them? Do they know that we treasure preaching the gospel of God to them? Do they know where our hearts are?

I have talked to some of the older folks in our congregation, and I think that the reason my predecessors are so honored is that, like Livingston, they preached the Word to a certain people in a certain time in a certain place. That Word did for those people in their land, in their time, what the Word always does—saves, changes lives, heals, restores, gives hope, brings assurance, and brings God to men and men to God. I am convinced that in the final analysis, this is the answer. All preachers, whether they consider themselves mice or elephants, great or small, are loved when they faithfully open up the Bread of Life and feed the lambs of Jesus. This becomes our legacy, not that our images are recorded in oils to hang on a church wall, but that our hearts are buried in that place where we took our stand, spent our years, and gave our lives to preach the Word. For, you see, to those whose lives are changed, you will always be a giant. Amen.

[24] An abbreviated story of Livingston's death and burial may be found at http://www.electricscotland.com/history/other/dlivingston.htm

[25] See *Livingstone's Last Journals in Central Africa*, 2 vols (1874), and *Missionary Travels (1857), Livingstone and the Explorers of Central Africa*, by Sir H. H. Johnston (1891), and *How I Found Livingstone*, by Sir H. M. Stanley (1872).

[26] Matthew 6:21